BASE 10 BLOCKS

Some pictures of the pieces are shown below.

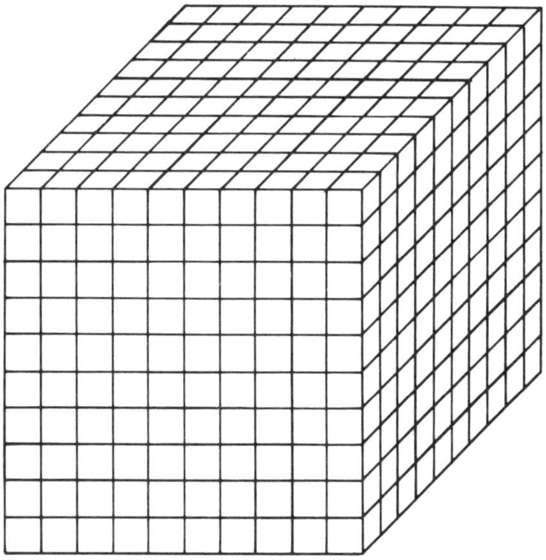

Name: _____

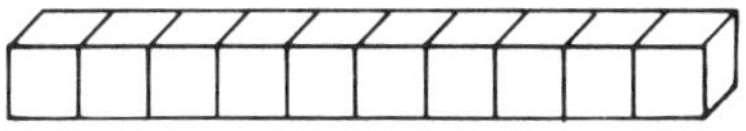

Name: _____

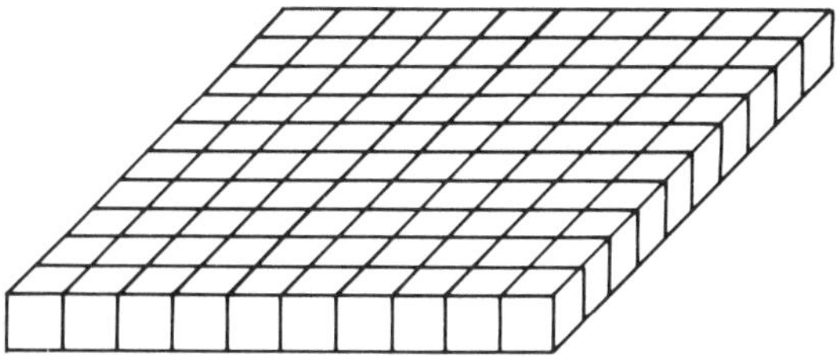

Name: _____

Name: _____

1. Can you find the smallest piece? Circle it.

2. Find the largest piece. Put an "L" (for "large") next to it.

3. Find the piece that looks like this ⬚⬚⬚⬚⬚⬚⬚⬚ . 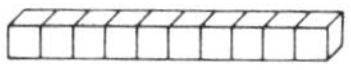
   Put an "X" on it.

4. Now locate the piece that looks like

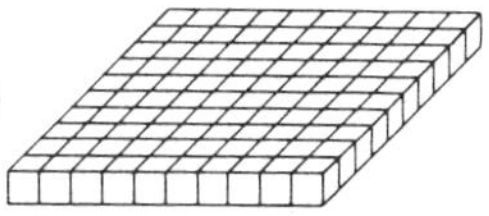

   Put a "_____" on it.

5. Give names to the pieces.

   For example, the ⬚ might be called "Stone."

   the ⬚⬚⬚ might be called "Brick."

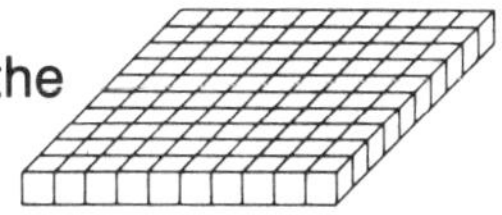

1

UNITS, UNITS, UNITS

Did you know that

has as much wood as

REMEMBER THIS FACT
10 UNITS have the same value as 1 ROD.

See if you can answer the questions below:

1. How many units? _____
   Circle ten units. Exchange the circled units for a rod.

   You now have _____ rods, _____ units.

2. How many units? _____
   Circle ten units. Exchange the circled units for a rod.

   You now have _____ rods, _____ units.

3. How many units? _____
   Circle ten units. Exchange the circled units for a rod.

   You now have _____ rods, _____ units.
   Circle another ten units. Exchange the circled units for a rod.

   You now have _____ rods, _____ units.

4. How many units? _____
   Circle ten units. Exchange the circled units for a rod.

   You now have _____ rods, _____ units.
   Circle another ten units. Exchange the circled units for a rod.

   You now have _____ rods, _____ units.

UNIT SETS

5. How many units? _____
   Circle ten units. Exchange the circled units for a rod.

   You now have _____ rods, _____ units.
   Circle another ten units.
      Exchange the circled units for a rod.

   You now have _____ rods, _____ units.
   Circle yet another ten units.
      Exchange the circled units for a rod.

   You now have _____ rods, _____ units.

6. How many units? _____
   Circle ten units. Exchange the circled units for a rod.

   You now have _____ rods, _____ units.
   Circle another ten units.
      Exchange the circled units for a rod.

   You now have _____ rods, _____ units.
   Circle yet another ten units.
      Exchange the circled units for a rod.

   You now have _____ rods, _____ units.

NOW IT'S YOUR TURN:
Try this activity again. This time you choose how many units. Make sure that each time you circle ten units, you make an exchange for a rod.

Remember the questions to ask?

   How many units? _____
   Circle ten units, exchange for one rod.

   You have _____ rods, _____ units.
   Can you circle another ten?

   If yes, you now have _____ rods, _____ units.

Repeat this until you cannot circle any more tens.
Keep a record of what you have done.

LET'S MAKE SOME TRADES

Start with:

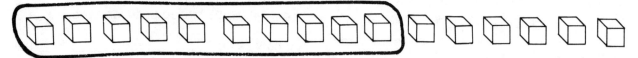

Let's make a chart to record our progress.

START WITH 16 UNITS

Number of Exchange	Now Have		Total Number of Units Exchanged
	Rods	Units	
1	1	6	10

Remember: Circle 10 units and exchange for a rod.

You try it:

Count out the number of units indicated.
Make exchanges and record your response on the chart.

The first one is started for you:

1. START WITH 33 UNITS

Number of Exchange	Now Have		Total Number of Units Exchanged
	Rods	Units	
1	1	23	10
2	2	13	20

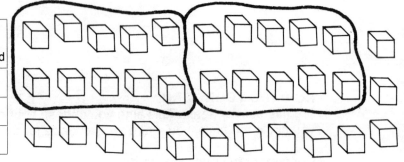

Now do one on your own:

2. START WITH 56 UNITS

Number of Exchange	Now Have		Total Number of Units Exchanged
	Rods	Units	
1			
2			
3			
4			
5			

TRADING EXPERIENCE

3. START WITH 65 UNITS

Number of Exchange	Now Have		Total Number of Units Exchanged
	Rods	Units	

4. START WITH 79 UNITS

Number of Exchange	Now Have		Total Number of Units Exchanged
	Rods	Units	

5. START WITH 87 UNITS

Number of Exchange	Now Have		Total Number of Units Exchanged
	Rods	Units	

6. START WITH 48 UNITS

Number of Exchange	Now Have		Total Number of Units Exchanged
	Rods	Units	

7. START WITH 50 UNITS

Number of Exchange	Now Have		Total Number of Units Exchanged
	Rods	Units	

AT THE TOY SHOP

Francoise's Toy Shop is quite unusual. All the toys are made of strangely shaped wood.
Each unit is worth one penny; each rod costs one dime. Can you help Francoise price his toys?

1. How many units can you fit into this shape? _____

Do any rods fit?_____
How many pennies would this shape cost? _____
What is the fewest number of coins you can use to pay for it?

_____ dimes, _____ pennies

3. How many units can you fit into this shape? _____

Do any rods fit?_____
How many pennies would this shape cost? _____

What is the fewest number of coins you can use to pay for it?

_____ dimes, _____ pennies

2. How many units can you fit into this shape? _____ Do any rods fit? _____

How many pennies would this shape cost?_____
What is the fewest number of coins you can use to pay for it?

_____ dimes, _____ pennies

5. How many units can you fit into this shape? _____

Do any rods fit? _____
How many pennies would this shape cost? _____

What is the fewest number of coins you can use to pay for it?

_____ dimes, _____ pennies

4. How many units can you fit into this shape? _____

Do any rods fit? _____
How many pennies would this shape cost? _____

What is the fewest number of coins you can use to pay for it?

_____ dimes, _____ pennies

COMPLETE THE CHARTS
The first two are done for you.

1. START WITH 57 UNITS

Number of Exchanges	Now Have		Total Number of Units Exchanged
	Rods	Units	
1	1	47	10
2	2	37	20
3	3	27	30
4	4	17	40
5	5	7	50

2. START WITH 42 UNITS

Number of Exchanges	Now Have		Total Number of Units Exchanged
	Rods	Units	
1	1	32	10
2	2	22	20
3	3	12	30
4	4	2	40

3. START WITH 39 UNITS

Number of Exchanges	Now Have		Total Number of Units Exchanged
	Rods	Units	

4. START WITH 54 UNITS

Number of Exchanges	Now Have		Total Number of Units Exchanged
	Rods	Units	

5. START WITH 81 UNITS

Number of Exchanges	Now Have		Total Number of Units Exchanged
	Rods	Units	

6. START WITH 46 UNITS

Number of Exchanges	Now Have		Total Number of Units Exchanged
	Rods	Units	

7. START WITH 78 UNITS

Number of Exchanges	Now Have		Total Number of Units Exchanged
	Rods	Units	

8. START WITH 93 UNITS

Number of Exchanges	Now Have		Total Number of Units Exchanged
	Rods	Units	

UNITS AND RODS

Helpful Helen was working with units and exchanging them for rods.
Can you help her fill in the chart. The first two are done for you.

Units Started With	Total Number of Units Exchanged	Now Have	
		Rods	Units
16	10	1	6
38	30	3	8
54			
47			
	60		7
		8	3
90			
	40		6
85			
		9	3
79			

LET'S GO FOR IT!!

Get a group of 3-5 friends together. Ask your teacher for a die and a collection of units and rods.

Each person should roll the die. The person with the highest roll goes first. The person with the lowest roll should be the banker.

Each player rolls the die and the banker gives him/her the number of units indicated on the die. As soon as possible, trade for a rod. You must make the exchange as soon as it is possible. If another player catches you with more than 10 units in your pile, you can be "sizzled" and all the units from your last roll must be returned to the banker.

The game ends when the first player gets five rods.

Want to make it more difficult? Try these variations:

1. You must figure out the exchange as soon as the die is rolled, and tell the other players BEFORE you can collect from the bank.

2. To win you must get EXACTLY five rods. Thus, if you have 4 rods, 6 units and roll a "5," you must forfeit your turn.

A BUILDING BREAK

It takes 10 units to make a rod. You collect units by rolling a die and taking the number of units indicated on the die.

For example,  is rolled; you would receive 4 units.

A) What is the smallest number you could roll?

B) What is the largest number you could roll?

C) If you wanted exactly one rod, what is the *smallest* number of rolls you could make? _____

Give two examples of combinations you could roll to do this. _____,_____ and _____,_____.

Are there any other rolls that would make this possible?

D) If you wanted exactly one rod, what is the *most* rolls you would have to make? _____

What number would you have to roll each time if this happened? _____

E) If it took 3 rolls to get a rod, what could you have rolled? _____ _____ _____

F) What about 4 rolls? _____ _____ _____ _____

G) What about 5 rolls? _____ _____ _____ _____ _____

Extra for Experts

H) If you were playing a game in which you must receive 5 flats to win, what would be the least number of rolls you would have to make?

TRADE

We can get the same amount of wood with a different number of pieces. Let's look below:

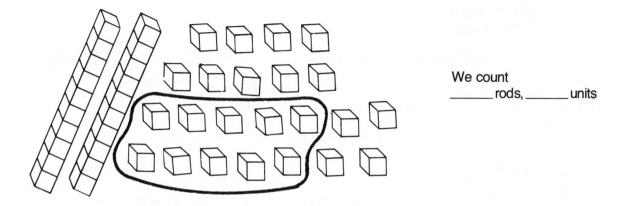

We count
_____ rods, _____ units

Exchanging 10 units for a rod does not change the amount of wood.

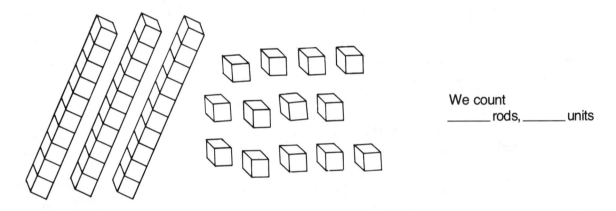

We count
_____ rods, _____ units

Exchanging yet another 10 units for a rod still does not change the amount of wood.

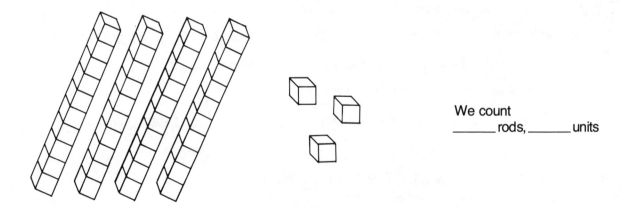

We count
_____ rods, _____ units

All three examples use the same amount of wood and have the same value.
Which way uses the fewest number of pieces?
Do you think this is the best way?   Why?
Do you think that the other ways could also be useful?

PICK THREE OTHER NUMBERS AND LOOK AT THE WAYS THEY CAN BE
REPRESENTED.

BACKWARD EXCHANGES

Backward Ben challenged Helpful Helen to a duel. He claimed that she couldn't exchange backwards. Helpful Helen bet that she could. Help her prove Backward Ben wrong!

Here's a sample:
START WITH 6 RODS, 5 UNITS

Number of Exchange	Total Number of Rods Exchanged	Now Have	
		Rods	Units
1	1	5	15
2	2	4	25
3	3	3	35
4	4	2	45
5	5	1	55
6	6	0	65

Now you try:

1. START WITH 5 RODS, 8 UNITS

Number of Exchange	Total Number of Rods Exchanged	Now Have	
		Rods	Units

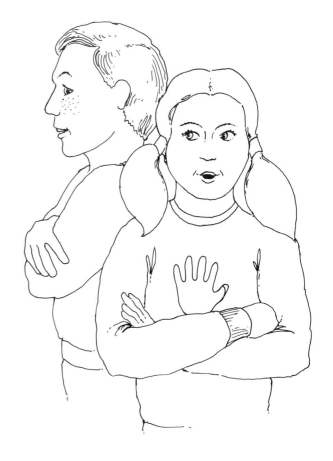

2. START WITH 4 RODS, 9 UNITS

Number of Exchange	Total Number of Rods Exchanged	Now Have	
		Rods	Units

COUNTING BACKWARD

3. START WITH 7 RODS, 1 UNIT

Number of Exchange	Total Number of Rods Exchanged	Now Have	
		Rods	Units

4. START WITH 6 RODS, 0 UNITS

Number of Exchange	Total Number of Rods Exchanged	Now Have	
		Rods	Units

5. START WITH 8 RODS, 3 UNITS

Number of Exchange	Total Number of Rods Exchanged	Now Have	
		Rods	Units

MEET THE FLAT

This piece is called a *FLAT*.
Can you find a block that looks like it? Draw its outline in the space below.

Does a rod fit inside the outline? _____ How many rods are needed to fill the shape?

You have filled the shape with rods. Therefore, one flat has the same value as _____ rods. If we exchange 1 rod for units, we will have _____ rods, _____ units. If we exchange a second rod for units we will have _____ rods, _____ units. NOW COMPLETE THIS CHART:

START WITH 1 FLAT, WHICH HAS THE SAME VALUE AS _____ RODS.

Total Number of Rods Exchanged	Now Have	
	Rods	Units

From our chart we see that 1 FLAT has the same value as _____ RODS.
Also, 1 FLAT is equivalent to _____ UNITS.

LET'S MAKE A TRADE

Start with:

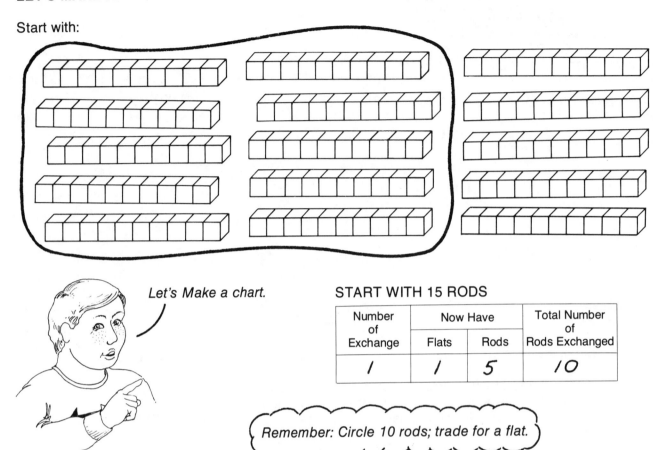

Let's Make a chart.

START WITH 15 RODS

Number of Exchange	Now Have		Total Number of Rods Exchanged
	Flats	Rods	
1	1	5	10

Remember: Circle 10 rods; trade for a flat.

You try! Count out a starting number of rods. Then make the necessary exchanges and record your response on the charts. The first one is started for you:

1. START WITH 22 RODS

Number of Exchange	Now Have		Total Number of Rods Exchanged
	Flats	Rods	
1	1	12	10

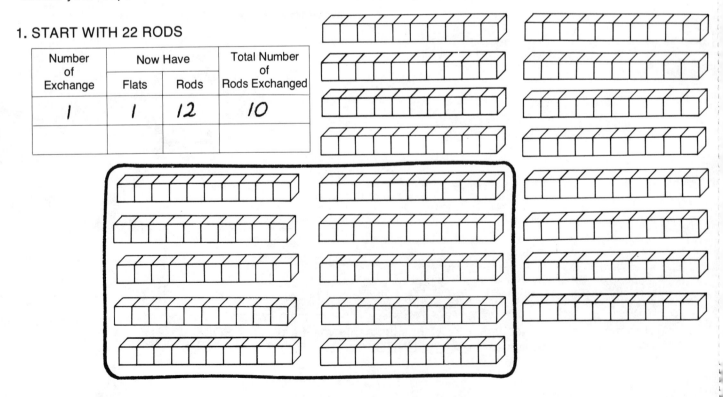

TRADING PRACTICE

2. START WITH 63 RODS

Number of Exchange	Now Have		Total Number of Rods Exchanged
	Flats	Rods	

3. START WITH 71 RODS

Number of Exchange	Now Have		Total Number of Rods Exchanged
	Flats	Rods	

4. START WITH 89 RODS

Number of Exchange	Now Have		Total Number of Rods Exchanged
	Flats	Rods	

5. START WITH 45 RODS

Number of Exchange	Now Have		Total Number of Rods Exchanged
	Flats	Rods	

6. START WITH 50 RODS

Number of Exchange	Now Have		Total Number of Rods Exchanged
	Flats	Rods	

Remember: 10 units have the same value as 1 rod.
10 rods are equivalent to 1 flat.

LET'S DO SOME EXCHANGES

START WITH 134 UNITS

Number of Exchange	Now Have			Total Number of Units Exchanged	Total Number of Rods Exchanged
	Flats	Rods	Units		
1	0	1	124	10	0
2	0	2	114	20	0
3	0	3	104	30	0
4	0	4	94	40	0
5	0	5	84	50	0
6	0	6	74	60	0
7	0	7	64	70	0
8	0	8	54	80	0
9	0	9	44	90	0
10	0	10	34	100	0
11	0	11	24	110	0
12	0	12	14	120	0
13	0	13	4	130	0
14	1	3	4	130	10

Now you try it!

1. START WITH 256 UNITS

Number of Exchange	Now Have			Total Number of Units Exchanged	Total Number of Rods Exchanged
	Flats	Rods	Units		

As you make your exchanges, check to see if a pattern developes. Use it to help you!

2. START WITH 325 UNITS

Number of Exchange	Now Have			Total Number of Units Exchanged	Total Number of Rods Exchanged
	Flats	Rods	Units		
			17		

3. START WITH 483 UNITS

Number of Exchange	Now Have			Total Number of Units Exchanged	Total Number of Rods Exchanged
	Flats	Rods	Units		

NUMBER PATTERNS

After completing several charts, Puzzler Pete noticed certain patterns emerging.

For example:
If he started with 257 units and exchanged these for rods, he ended up with 25 rods, 7 units. If the rods were then exchanged for flats, he had 2 flats, 5 rods, 7 units.

He reasoned that if he started with 362 units, he would end up with 3 flats, 6 rods and 2 units.

Help him confirm his theory by filling in the spaces below:

Number of Units to Start With	Exchange for Rods Now Have		Exchange for Flats Now Have		
	Rods	Units	Flats	Rods	Units
275					
463					
782					
603					
526					
419					
378					
487					
136					
283					

Which exchange allows you to state the value of the block using the fewest number of pieces.

Eager Eddie decided to be helpful by erasing all the answers Helpful Helen had filled in on the chart below. Luckily, he left some spaces untouched. Can you help figure out what should go in the empty spaces.

Units Start With	Total Number of Units Exchanged	Total Number of Rods Exchanged	Now Have		
			Flats	Rods	Units
35	30	0	0	3	5
235	230	20	2	3	5
143					
367					7
	450				
			5	4	9
307					
	630				0
98					
			1	8	2
	40				3
596					

CONVERSIONS

Given the number of units shown in Column 1: If you could make no more exchanges, how would the other columns be filled out? Record the results below:

Number of Units	Flats	Rods	Units
45			
99			
35			
321			
903			
400			
563			
89			
657			
835			
198			
387			
742			
946			
849			

LET'S PLAY A GAME

Gather a group of 3-5 friends together. Ask your teacher for 2 dice (each a different color) and a collection of flats, rods and units.

Each player rolls a die. The person with the highest roll goes first. The player with the lowest roll becomes the banker.

Players determine which die represents rods, which represents units. Each player rolls the dice, in turn, and collects the rods and units won. Player may not collect units or rods if the addition means that the player will have more than 10 of a kind in his or her pile. Extras must be exchanged immediately with the roll.

[For example, if a player has 7 rods, 6 units in his or her pile and rolls 4 rods, 3 units, the units may be collected, but 6 rods must be given to the banker and a flat collected.]

It is the banker's job to insure that exchanges are done properly. When the first player collects 5 flats, the game ends.

Want to make it more difficult? Try these variations:
1. Have the pair of dice represent units only.
2. The players must collect *exactly* 5 flats to win. Thus, if you have 4 flats, 8 rods, 3 units and roll 3 rods, 6 units...you may take the 6 units, but forfeit the 3 rods.

MEET THE CUBE

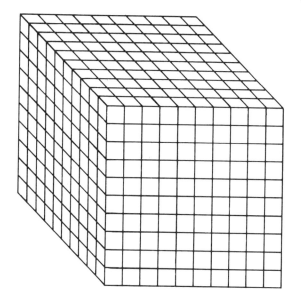

This piece is called a CUBE.
Can you find a block that looks like it?
Set it down in front of you.

Place a flat on top of the cube. Does it fit exactly? Now place the flat next to the cube and stack more flats on top. How many flats must be stacked to reach the same height as the cube? _____ Therefore, we can say _____ flats have the same value as _____ cube.

If you exchanged a flat for rods, you would have _____ flats _____ rods.

Complete the chart:

Number of Flats Exchanged	Now Have	
	Flats	Rods
1		

Thus, we can say that one cube has the same value as _____ flats, also 1 cube is equivalent to _____ rods.

Let's continue and trade for units. Use the chart on the next page for this activity. How many units do you think it will take to make a cube? (Make a guess. Record it then make the exchanges necessary. When you finish the chart, see how close you were.)

_____

EXPLORING THE CUBE

START WITH 1 CUBE

Flats	Rods	Units
10	0	0
9	10	0
8	20	0
7	30	0
6	40	0
5	50	0
4	60	0
3	70	0
2	80	0
1	90	0
0	100	0
0	99	10
0	98	20
0	97	30
0		
0		
0		
0		
0		
0	0	
0		
0		
0		
0		
0	3	970
0	2	980
0	1	990
0	0	1000

22

EXCHANGING FLATS

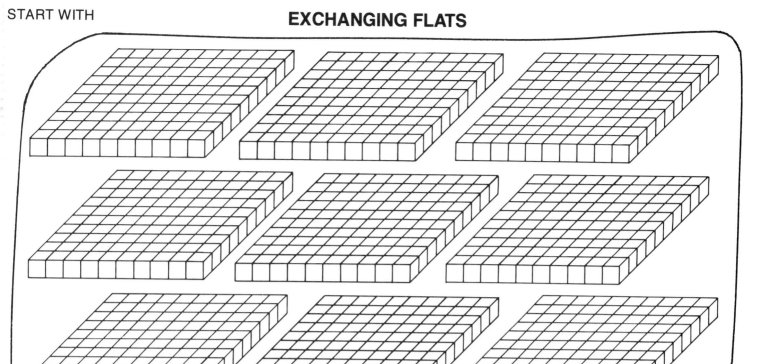

1. START WITH 12 FLATS

Number of Exchange	Now Have		Total Number of Flats Exchanged
	Cube	Flat	

 Now you try:

Remember 10 flats have the same value as 1 cube

2. START WITH 24 FLATS

Number of Exchange	Now Have		Total Number of Flats Exchanged
	Cube	Flat	

EXCHANGING MORE FLATS

3. START WITH 67 FLATS

Number of Exchange	Now Have		Total Number of Flats Exchanged
	Cubes	Flats	

4. START WITH 70 FLATS

Number of Exchange	Now Have		Total Number of Flats Exchanged
	Cubes	Flats	

5. START WITH 81 FLATS

Number of Exchange	Now Have		Total Number of Flats Exchanged
	Cubes	Flats	

6. START WITH 84 FLATS

Number of Exchange	Now Have		Total Number of Flats Exchanged
	Cubes	Flats	

7. START WITH 53 FLATS

Number of Exchange	Now Have		Total Number of Flats Exchanged
	Cubes	Flats	

Remember 10 flats have the same value as 1 cube.
Also, 10 rods are equivalent to 1 flat.

LET'S EXCHANGE.

START WITH 119 RODS

Number of Exchange	Now Have			Total Number of Rods Exchanged	Total Number of Flats Exchanged
	Cubes	Flats	Rods		
1	0	1	109	10	0
2	0	2	99	20	0
3	0	3	89	30	0
4	0	4	79	40	0
5	0	5	69	50	0
6	0	6	59	60	0
7	0	7	49	70	0
8	0	8	39	80	0
9	0	9	29	90	0
10	0	10	19	100	0
11	0	11	9	110	0
12	1	1	9	110	10

Study the chart.
Check to see if any patterns exist.
Use them to help you make exchanges!

Now you try:

1. START WITH 235 RODS

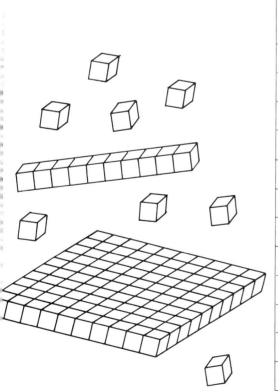

Number of Exchange	Now Have			Total Number of Rods Exchanged	Total Number of Flats Exchanged
	Cubes	Flats	Rods		

EXCHANGE SOME MORE

2. START WITH 346 RODS

Number of Exchange	Now Have			Total Number of Rods Exchanged	Total Number of Flats Exchanged
	Cubes	Flats	Rods		

3. START WITH 438 RODS

Number of Exchange	Now Have			Total Number of Rods Exchanged	Total Number of Flats Exchanged
	Cubes	Flats	Rods		

ERASED!

In his eagerness to clean, Eager Eddie has done it again. He erased almost all the answers Helpful Helen had filled in below. Lucky for you, he was caught before he finished.

Help figure out what should go in the empty spaces.

Number of Rods Started With	Total Number of Rods Exchanged	Total Number of Flats Exchanged	Now Have		
			Cubes	Flats	Rods
46	40	0	0	4	6
324	320	30	3	2	4
234					
278					
	360				8
			6	3	7
506					
	740				0
			2	7	3
	50				4
			5	9	6
458					

COMPLETE THE CHART

Puzzler Pierre studied all the charts you have carefully completed. He observed certain patterns occurring.

If he started with 1,234 units and exchanged as many rods as he could, there would be 123 rods, 4 units. If he then traded the rods for as many flats as he could, he would have 12 flats, 3 rods, 4 units. Finally, if he traded the flats for cubes, he would have 1 cube, 2 flats, 3 rods, 4 units.

It was clear to him that the same value of the wood could be given in many different ways depending upon the number of pieces used.

Let's put his idea to work by filling in the chart below:

Start With This Number of Units	Exchange for Rods Now Have		Exchange for Flats Now Have			Exchange for Cube Now Have			
	Rods	Units	Flats	Rods	Units	Cubes	Flats	Rods	Units
1364									
2375									
1693									
2360									
3457									
1409									
4372									
2437									
634									
4361									

CONSTRUCT THESE NUMBERS

Given the number of units in Column 1, what would you end up with if you could make no more exchanges? Record your results on the chart below:

Number of Units	Cubes	Flats	Rods	Units
1345				
299				
3275				
1321				
804				
3700				
2654				
498				
1078				
3568				
924				
1196				
2837				
2310				
3247				

LET'S PLAY A GAME

Name: *BREAK THE CUBE*

Objective: To exchange all of your blocks until none are left.

Number of Players: 3-5 (One player acts as banker).

Materials Needed: A pair of different colored dice; a cube for each player; units, rods, and flats

Play: One die represents units; the other represents rods. Each player rolls the dice and pays the banker the number of rods and units indicated. Play continues until one player has no more pieces.

ALL IN THE BOTTOM

Look at the number of unit blocks in the first rectangle.
Now look at the number of unit blocks in the second rectangle.
Place unit blocks over the pictures on this page. If you combine all the pieces in the bottom rectangle, how many will you have in all?

The first one is started for you.

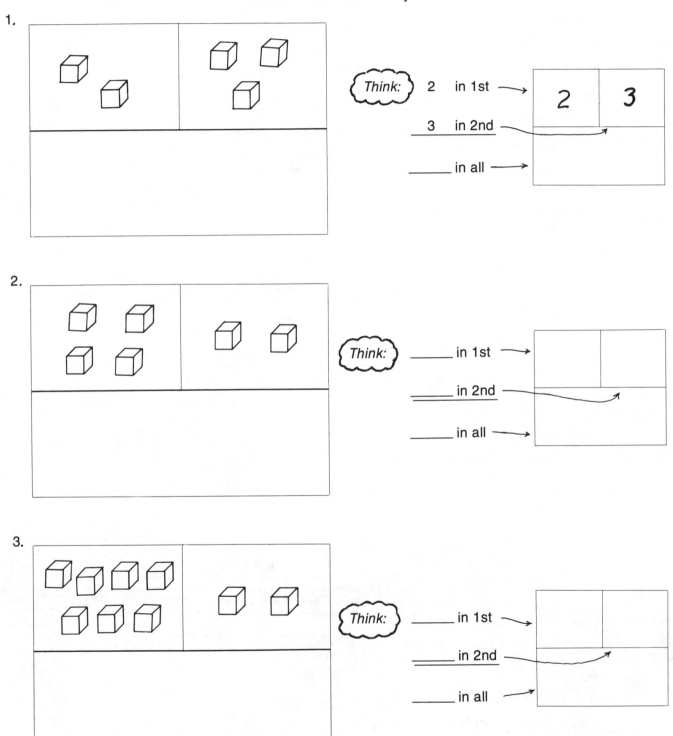

1.

Think: 2   in 1st →   [2 | 3]
          3   in 2nd
_____ in all →

2.

Think: _____ in 1st →
          _____ in 2nd →
          _____ in all →

3.

Think: _____ in 1st →
          _____ in 2nd →
          _____ in all →

FACT RECTANGLES

Let's make it a little more difficult:
Look at the number of units in the 1st rectangle. Record the number in the space provided. Do the same for the 2nd rectangle. If you move all the units into the bottom rectangle, how many would you have? Record any exchanges necessary. These rectangles are called fact rectangles.

1.

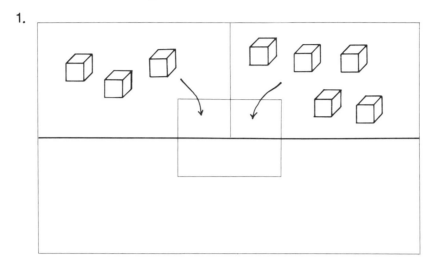

2.

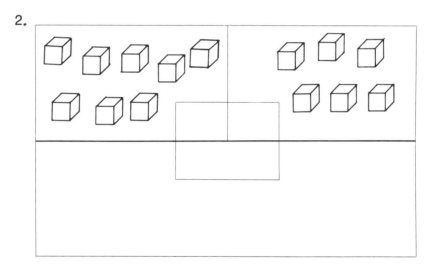

3.

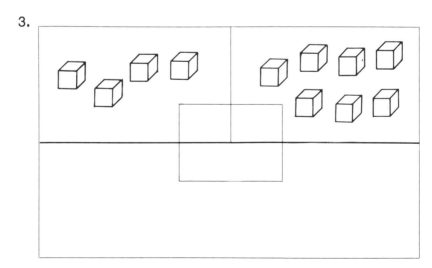

MORE FACT RECTANTLES

Ask your teacher to provide you with a fact rectangle. Then get a handful of units and rods. Put them in a container. Reach into the container and remove some blocks. Put them in the first rectangle. Record the number you have drawn in the space provided. Then make any exchanges you can. Do the same for the second rectangle. Move everything into the bottom rectangle. Make any exchanges you can to have the same value with the smallest number of pieces.

Eager Eddie has done a sample for you.

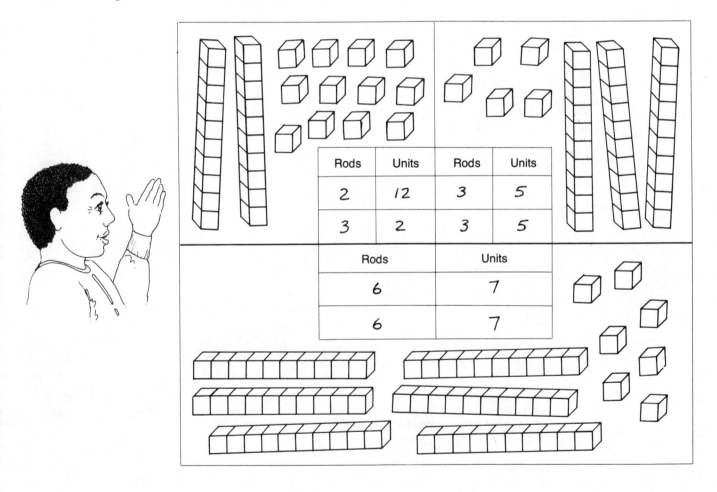

Rods	Units	Rods	Units
2	12	3	5
3	2	3	5

Rods	Units
6	7
6	7

COMBINE COLLECTIONS

Eager Eddie and Helpful Helen were working together. Eager Eddie reached into the collection box and pulled out 3 cubes, 4 flats, 13 rods, and 12 units. He made the exchanges necessary to get the same value using the least amount of wood and recorded the result in the chart below. Helpful Helen then reached in and pulled out 1 cube, 15 flats, 6 rods and 14 units. She also made exchanges and recorded her results.

Let's look at these:

	Cubes	Flats	Rods	Units
Eddie	3	5	4	2
Helen	2	5	7	4
Total	5	10	11	6
Exchanges	1	1		
Total After Exchange	6	1	1	6

They decided to combine their collections.

We can make some exchanges so that we can show the same value using the fewest number of pieces.

Let's do it again:
Look at what Eddie and Helen have picked.
Duplicate with your Base 10 Blocks.
Figure out the total, using the fewest number of pieces.

	Cubes	Flats	Rods	Units
Eddie	1	4	6	3
Helen	3	8	2	7
Total				
Exchanges				
Total After Exchange				

Exchange for the same value, using the fewest number of pieces.

COMBINING THE BLOCKS

For this activity you need two students to duplicate the game played by Eager Eddie and Helpful Helen on the preceding pages.

Let's review the steps:

1. Student A goes to the collection box and (with eyes closed) picks out cubes, flats, rods and units.
2. Make any exchanges necessary to represent the amount picked with the fewest number of pieces.
3. Record your amount.
4. Student B perform Steps 1, 2, 3.
5. See how much Student A and Student B has in all.
6. Make exchanges to represent the amount using the fewest number of pieces.

Do this activity about 10 times. Share your solutions with your teacher when you have completed them.

1.

Name	Cubes	Flats	Rods	Units
Total				
Exchange				
Total After Exchange				

2.

Name	Cubes	Flats	Rods	Units
Total				
Exchange				
Total After Exchange				

3.

Name	Cubes	Flats	Rods	Units
Total				
Exchange				
Total After Exchange				

4.

Name	Cubes	Flats	Rods	Units
Total				
Exchange				
Total After Exchange				

WANT A CHALLENGE?
Try this activity with 3 students; then 4 students together.

CHECK THE TOTALS

Eager Eddie and Helpful Helen had a lot of fun putting their collections together to see how many they had in all. The results of their collections and the totals are below. Check to see if they are correct. If they are not—see if you can correct them.

1.

Name	Cubes	Flats	Rods	Units
Eddie	2	7	9	8
Sally	3	8	6	5
Total	5	15	15	13
Total After Exchanges	5	6	5	3

Record any corrections needed here:

Cubes	Flats	Rods	Units

2.

Name	Cubes	Flats	Rods	Units
Eddie	3	4	5	2
Sally	5	6	4	8
Total	8	10	9	10
Total After Exchange	8	1	0	0

Record any corrections needed here:

Cubes	Flats	Rods	Units

3.

Name	Cubes	Flats	Rods	Units
Eddie	2	5	7	4
Sally	4	9	3	8
Total	6	14	10	12
Total After Exchange	7	5	1	2

Record any corrections needed here:

Cubes	Flats	Rods	Units

FIND THE TOTAL

Let's look at some more of Eager Eddie's and Helpful Helen's record sheets. This time you total them and make the necessary exchanges necessary to represent the value using the fewest number of pieces.

1.

Name	Cubes	Flats	Rods	Units
Eddie	5	7	9	6
Helen	2	4	7	8
Total				
Total After Exchange				

2.

Name	Cubes	Flats	Rods	Units
Eddie	3	1	6	8
Helen	5	7	3	9
Total				
Total After Exchange				

3.

Name	Cubes	Flats	Rods	Units
Eddie	4	5	9	7
Helen	1	8	6	4
Total				
Total After Exchange				

4.

Name	Cubes	Flats	Rods	Units
Eddie	3	1	8	4
Helen	6	2	3	5
Total				
Total After Exchange				

PRACTICE COMBINING THE BLOCKS

On the next few pages are copies of students record sheets. We have left off the names to protect the innocent! See if you can figure out how many in all and make the exchanges necessary to represent the value using the fewest number of pieces.

1.

	Cubes	Flats	Rods	Units
	3	6	9	4
	2	8	5	7
Total				
Total After Exchange				

2.

	Cubes	Flats	Rods	Units
	3	5	7	6
	2	3	4	9
Total				
Total After Exchange				

3.

	Cubes	Flats	Rods	Units
	6	5	8	7
	2	4	8	6
Total				
Total After Exchange				

4.

	Cubes	Flats	Rods	Units
	5	3	7	6
	3	6	1	5
Total				
Total After Exchange				

5.

	Cubes	Flats	Rods	Units
	7	8	4	6
	1	8	4	6
Total				
Total After Exchange				

6.

	Cubes	Flats	Rods	Units
	6	3	9	2
	1	5	4	7
Total				
Total After Exchange				

MORE PRACTICE COMBINING THE BLOCKS

1.

	Cubes	Flats	Rods	Units
	5	7	6	8
	3	1	2	4
Total				
Total After Exchange				

2.

	Cubes	Flats	Rods	Units
	3	9	8	5
	2	4	6	7
Total				
Total After Exchange				

3.

	Cubes	Flats	Rods	Units
	8	2	8	5
	1	3	9	5
Total				
Total After Exchange				

4.

	Cubes	Flats	Rods	Units
	4	9	7	4
	3	8	7	6
Total				
Total After Exchange				

5.

	Cubes	Flats	Rods	Units
	6	7	9	3
	4	8	2	6
Total				
Total After Exchange				

6.

	Cubes	Flats	Rods	Units
	5	8	6	1
	4	7	3	9
Total				
Total After Exchange				

MORE COMBINING THE BLOCKS

Helpful Helen and Eager Eddie were sitting and discussing their new game of combining their blocks. Here is their record sheet. Let's look at it and eavesdrop on their conversation.

"Look, Helen, we have 11 rods. We can exchange 10 rods for a flat."

	Cubes	Flats	Rods	Units
Eddie	3	5	4	2
Helen	2	8	7	4
Total	5	13	11	6

"But Eddie, now we have 14 flats. We need to exchange 10 of the flats for a cube."

	Cubes	Flats	Rods	Units
This gives us:	5	14	1	6

"When we had 11 rods we could tell immediately that they were going to be 1 rod, 1 flat."

	Cubes	Flats	Rods	Units
This gives us:	6	4	1	6

"Oh, yes! and the 13 flats are the same value as 3 flats, 1 cube."

	Cubes	Flats	Rods	Units
When we first combined, we had	5	13	11	6

"I have a neat idea! You had 2 units, I had 4 units...together we had 6 units. We could make no exchanges—so I'm going to record that *below* the double lines I drew."

"However, you had 4 rods, I had 7 rods. Combined, this gives us 11 rods. We exchange 10 of these for 1 flat, which gives us 1 flat, 1 rod. I'll record this by putting a "1" in the rod column *below* the double line and a "1" in the flat column above the double line."

	Cubes	Flats	Rods	Units
Eddie	3	5	4	2
Helen	2	8	7	4
			1	
			1	6

39

Oh! I get it!
I had 5 flats, you had 8, plus we have 1 more from the exchange we made. This would give us 14 flats, 10 of which we can exchange for 1 cube. We record this by putting the 4 *below* the double line in the flats column and the 1 *above* the double line in the cube column.

	Cubes	Flats	Rods	Units
Eddie	3	5	4	2
Helen	2	8	7	4
Exchange	1	1		
Result		4	1	6

Yeah, and now we have 6 cubes—3 from you, 2 from me and 1 we got from exchanging the flats.

	Cubes	Flats	Rods	Units
Eddie	3	5	4	2
Helen	2	8	7	4
Exchange	1	1		
Result	6	4	1	6

Let's do it again:
Look at what Eddie and Helen have chosen. Duplicate what they have done with your wooden pieces. Figure out how many they will have after combining their draws.

	Cubes	Flats	Rods	Units
Eddie	1	4	6	3
Helen	3	8	2	7
Exchange			1	
Result				0

We started for you—
You finish.

CHECK THE EXPERTS

Eager Eddie and Helpful Helen found the answer sheets below in a stack on their teacher's desk. They like the idea of the shortcut they discovered. Check their work below and make any corrections necessary.

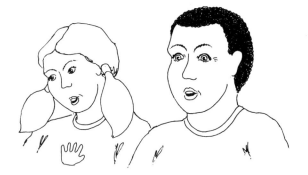

1.

Cubes	Flats	Rods	Units
2	6	7	5
3	6	9	4
1			
6	2	6	9

Make corrections here:

2.

Cubes	Flats	Rods	Units
4	2	7	6
4	7	8	9
1	1	1	
9	0	6	5

Make corrections here:

3.

Cubes	Flats	Rods	Units
3	7	4	3
5	7	6	8
1	1		
8	5	0	1

Make corrections here:

TRY THE SHORTCUT

Try using Helpful Helen and Eager Eddie's shortcut on these problems.

1.

Cubes	Flats	Rods	Units
1	9	4	8
7	9	7	9

2.

Cubes	Flats	Rods	Units
6	8	9	3
1	7	8	6

3.

Cubes	Flats	Rods	Units
2	7	9	6
3	8	4	7

4.

Cubes	Flats	Rods	Units
7	6	5	4
2	1	3	8

5.

Cubes	Flats	Rods	Units
3	5	6	9
4	9	8	5

6.

Cubes	Flats	Rods	Units
6	4	3	0
3	6	3	8

7.

Cubes	Flats	Rods	Units
4	3	0	6
7	8	9	4

8.

Cubes	Flats	Rods	Units
5	2	9	7
8	7	4	7

PRACTICE

Here are some more problems. They got lazy and left off the headings.

1.

2	8	3	5
5	9	6	8

2.

7	9	8	4
1	8	9	7

3.

3	8	4	6
2	6	9	7

4.

8	7	4	6
1	2	4	8

5.

4	6	7	8
5	8	9	6

6.

5	3	4	0
2	9	4	7

7.

3	4	0	5
8	9	4	5

8.

4	1	8	6
6	8	3	6

MORE PRACTICE

Eager Eddie and Helpful Helen found these problems. At first they were puzzled but Eddie assured Helen that as long as they did the exchanges and kept the numbers in line, they could imagine the boxes.

The first one is done for you:

	3	6	5	4
	2	8	7	3
	1	1	1	
	6	5	3	3

Now you're on your own. Remember to keep the numbers in line.

1.
```
  4  5  6  2
  1  9  6  7
_____
```

2.
```
  3  6  9  1
  4  8  2  8
_____
```

3.
```
  2  5  8  4
  1  9  7  3
_____
```

4.
```
  4  9  5  7
  3  7  8  6
_____
```

5.
```
  6  4  5  1
  3  8  5  8
_____
```

6.
```
  9  8  5  7
  1  8  6  9
_____
```

7.
```
  4  5  0  6
  2  9  3  5
_____
```

8.
```
  4  0  7  8
  6  9  0  8
_____
```

FILL THE GAPS

Eager Eddie and Helpful Helen were particularly upset. It seems that Puzzler Pierre had come by and erased some of their records. Help them by figuring out the values of the missing pieces.

1.

Cubes	Flats	Rods	Units
4	8	2	9
3	7		1
1		1	
	5	8	0

2.

Cubes	Flats	Rods	Units
5	2	1	4
	7		
1	1	1	
9	0	8	3

3.

Cubes	Flats	Rods	Units
2	7	1	9
4		8	6
7	6	0	5

4.

Cubes	Flats	Rods	Units
6	7	3	9
2		5	7
1			
9	5		

5.

Cubes	Flats	Rods	Units
7	4	5	4
1		4	
		1	
8	7	0	2

6.

Cubes	Flats	Rods	Units
	8		5
4	6	5	7
1		1	
7	4	9	

7.

Cubes	Flats	Rods	Units
4	0	6	1
	7		
	1		
6	8	5	2

8.

Cubes	Flats	Rods	Units
3	7		8
		6	9
1	1		
6	6	4	7

PATCH UP THESE CHARTS

Puzzler Pierre got even more daring with these problems. See if you can patch things up by supplying the values of the missing pieces.

1.

5	7	8	9
	2	7	
1	1		
7	0		4

2.

6	3	2	5
	6		
9		2	3

3.

4		6	2
	4		9
6	0	5	1

4.

5		1	5
	4		8
8	3	5	3

5.

4	8	6	4
3			6
	0	4	

6.

4	0	3	2
4			8
	0	0	

7.

5	4	1	2
9	1	7	1

8.

3	7	2	6
6	1	7	1

46

GO FOR BROKE

Eager Eddie and Helpful Helen invented a new game to play.

They made a spinner which looked like this:

The game began by spinning the spinner and by rolling a pair of dice. (One red die represents the number of rods, the white die represents units). If the spinner landed on "Give," the player would give the number of rods and units indicated on the dice to the other player. If the spinner landed on "Take," the player takes the number of rods and units indicated on the dice from the other player. If the spinner pointed to "Bank,"—the amount of the dice roll was forfeited to the Bank.

Each started with 10 rods and kept a record of each turn. The first player who went "broke" would lose.

Let's look at Eager Eddie's Record Sheet for his first 5 turns.

Spin 1—GIVE

	Rods	Units
Started	10	
Give	6	3
Left	3	7

Spin 2—TAKE

	Rods	Units
Started	3	7
Take	5	6
Left	9	3

Spin 3—BANK

	Rods	Units
Started	9	3
Bank	4	2
Left	5	1

Spin 4—GIVE

	Rods	Units
Started	5	1
Give	3	6
Left	1	5

Spin 5—TAKE

	Rods	Units
Started	1	5
Take	6	4
Left	7	9

Now see if you can figure out Helpful Helen's moves:

Spin 1—BANK

	Rods	Units
Start	10	
Bank	3	2
Left		

Spin 2—GIVE

	Rods	Units
Start		
Give	1	6
Left		

Spin 3—TAKE

	Rods	Units
Start		
Take	5	3
Left		

Spin 4—GIVE

	Rods	Units
Start		
Give	4	6
Left		

Spin 5—BANK

	Rods	Units
Start		
Bank	4	3
Left		

If you did everything correctly, you should have 1 rod, 6 units left.

MORE "GO FOR BROKE"

Helpful Helen and Eager Eddie decided to play until one of them "went broke." Let's see if you can figure out the results of each spin.

EDDIE
Spin 6—BANK

	Rods	Units
Start	7	9
Bank	3	6
Left		

HELEN
Spin 6—TAKE

	Rods	Units
Start	1	6
Take	4	5
Left		

Spin 7—TAKE

	Rods	Units
Start		
Take	2	6
Left		

Spin 7—TAKE

	Rods	Units
Start		
Take	3	1
Left		

Spin 8—BANK

	Rods	Units
Start		
Bank	4	4
Left		

Spin 8—GIVE

	Rods	Units
Start		
Give	2	4
Left		

Spin 9—GIVE

	Rods	Units
Start		
Give	3	1
Left		

Spin 9—BANK

	Rods	Units
Start		
Bank	1	6
Left		

Spin 9 caused someone to "go broke." Who was it? _____

A NEW GAME

Helpful Helen and Eager Eddie really enjoyed the new game and decided to expand on it. They kept the "action" spinner, but added 3 spinners, numbered 1-9 to represent units, rods and flats. They gave themselves 9 flats, 9 rods and 9 units to start.

 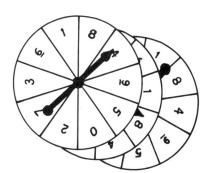

Let's see what Helen's first 4 spins were:

Spin 1—BANK

	Flats	Rods	Units
Start	9	9	9
Bank	6	4	5
Left	3	5	4

Spin 2—TAKE

	Flats	Rods	Units
Start	3	5	4
Take	5	6	9
Left	9	2	3

Figure the results!

Spin 3—GIVE

	Flats	Rods	Units
Start	9	2	3
Give	3	8	1
Left			

Spin 4—TAKE

	Flats	Rods	Units
Start			
Take	2	5	7
Left			

Let's take a look at some other rolls—you tell the result.

1.

Eddie	Flats	Rods	Units
Start	8	5	2
Bank	3	7	4
Left			

2.

Helen	Flats	Rods	Units
Start	6	4	8
Give	5	9	3
Left			

3.

Eddie	Flats	Rods	Units
Start	3	8	5
Take	4	3	7
Left			

4.

Helen	Flats	Rods	Units
Start	5	8	1
Bank	3	7	9
Left			

CUBES INCLUDED

Helpful Helen and Eager Eddie wanted to see what would happen if they expanded their game to include cubes. They knew that they really couldn't collect or give away cubes because they didn't have enough wooden pieces. So they decided to use strips of paper to represent the 9 cubes they wanted to start with. They now used 4 spinners, numbered 0-9 to represent units, rods, flats, and cubes as well as the action spinner. They started with 9 cubes, 9 flats, 9 rods and 9 units.

Let's see what Eddie's first 4 spins were like:

Spin 1—GIVE

	Cubes	Flats	Rods	Units
Start	9	9	9	9
Give	5	4	6	8
Left	4	5	3	1

Spin 2—TAKE

	Cubes	Flats	Rods	Units
Start	4	5	3	1
Take	4	6	7	8
Left	9	2	0	9

You figure the results.

Spin 3—BANK

	Cubes	Flats	Rods	Units
Start	9	2	0	9
Bank	4	1	3	7
Left				

Spin 4—TAKE

	Cubes	Flats	Rods	Units
Start				
Take	3	2	6	8
Left				

Let's look at some other rolls; you record the result.

1.

Eddie	Cubes	Flats	Rods	Units
Start	6	9	6	3
Bank	4	4	8	5
Left				

2.

Helen	Cubes	Flats	Rods	Units
Start	7	5	3	7
Give	4	4	8	2
Left				

3.

Eddie	Cubes	Flats	Rods	Units
Start	7	4	9	6
Take	2	5	4	8
Left				

4.

Helen	Cubes	Flats	Rods	Units
Start	5	6	9	2
Bank	4	4	8	9
Left				

EXCHANGE, EXCHANGE, EXCHANGE!

Eager Eddie was faced with this situation:

He looked at the cubes and thought that was OK; if he gave 2 away he still had 2. He could give 5 flats away because that would leave him with 1. But he was stopped when he looked at the rods:

	Cubes	Flats	Rods	Units
Started	4	6	8	5
Give	2	5	9	7

"I have to give away more than I started with! I know, I'll make an exchange!!"

	Cubes	Flats	Rods	Units
Started	4	5	18	5
Give	2	5	9	7

"Oh, NO! I have the same situation with units. I'll need to make another exchange."

	Cubes	Flats	Rods	Units
Started	4	5	17	15
Give	2	5	9	7

"Now everything works because I have the same value I began with, but I have enough of each piece to give away."

Can you make some exchanges so that in each situation below you keep the same value as you started with, but you have enough of each piece to give away? Use your blocks to help you! Make a record of your exchanges.

1.

Cubes	Flats	Rods	Units
5	7	4	6
4	3	6	8

2.

Cubes	Flats	Rods	Units
6	4	5	4
3	8	9	6

3.

Cubes	Flats	Rods	Units
4	2	0	7
3	8	3	8

4.

Cubes	Flats	Rods	Units
6	7	5	4
3	9	8	7

PRACTICE SUBTRACTING

You're doing great. Only now, after you make the exchanges, tell how much will be left! Don't forget to make a record of your exchanges.

1.

	Cubes	Flats	Rods	Units
Started	7	3	5	8
Give	4	5	7	9
Left				

2.

	Cubes	Flats	Rods	Units
Started	5	2	0	4
Give	3	7	1	9
Left				

3.

	Cubes	Flats	Rods	Units
Started	6	7	6	4
Give	2	9	5	8
Left				

4.

	Cubes	Flats	Rods	Units
Started	4	0	3	5
Give	3	2	6	7
Left				

5.

	Cubes	Flats	Rods	Units
Started	7	3	4	5
Give	5	8	7	9
Left				

6.

	Cubes	Flats	Rods	Units
Started	6	4	7	2
Give	4	2	9	8
Left				

7.

	Cubes	Flats	Rods	Units
Started	5	7	9	0
Give	1	9	3	7
Left				

BORROWING

Helpful Helen approached Eager Eddie with a suggestion:

"Eddie, instead of copying your records over and over, how about making your exchanges right above your original value. Let me show you what I mean!"

	Cubes	Flats	Rods	Units
	4	12	11	16
Start	5	3	2	6
Give	2	4	5	9

You need to make exchanges for flats, rods and units. Think about what the exchange will be and record it above the amount you started with. Notice there are not enough units or rods or flats so we exchange 1 cube, leaving us with 4, which we enter above the '5'. Now we have 13 flats, but we need to exchange one of these so we enter a 12 above the "3" in the flats column. This gives us 12 rods, but we need to exchange one of these for units. We enter 11 above the '2' in the rods column and 16 above the '6' in units. We still have the same value but now we have enough of each piece to give away.

Here, you try it. Just make the exchange necessary. But be careful! Sometimes an exchange will not be necessary. For example, look at:

Here we need to make exchanges for units and flats, but *not* for rods. Be careful!

	Cubes	Flats	Rods	Units
	3	13	5	13
Start	4	3	6	3
Give	1	8	4	6

Now you are on your own:

1.

	Cubes	Flats	Rods	Units
Start	6	7	6	5
Give	4	3	9	7

2.

	Cubes	Flats	Rods	Units
Start	5	3	7	0
Give	4	8	9	4

3.

	Cubes	Flats	Rods	Units
Start	5	2	7	1
Give	1	3	4	9

4.

	Cubes	Flats	Rods	Units
Start	4	0	3	0
Give	2	2	8	7

5.

	Cubes	Flats	Rods	Units
Start	7	6	5	4
Give	4	9	6	8

6.

	Cubes	Flats	Rods	Units
Start	6	5	0	4
Give	2	9	3	8

7.

	Cubes	Flats	Rods	Units
Start	8	9	2	0
Give	3	6	5	1

8.

	Cubes	Flats	Rods	Units
Start	7	4	8	6
Give	3	6	8	9

WHAT REMAINS

Try using Helpful Helen's technique to find out what remains. Notice Helen uses the notation (−) to indicate that she wants to give away the bottom amount.

1.

Cubes	Flats	Rods	Units
5	7	6	4
− 3	5	8	6

2.

Cubes	Flats	Rods	Units
8	6	4	3
− 5	7	8	2

3.

Cubes	Flats	Rods	Units
7	5	7	3
− 3	6	7	7

4.

Cubes	Flats	Rods	Units
6	0	7	4
− 4	8	5	8

5.

Cubes	Flats	Rods	Units
6	7	0	7
− 4	8	9	4

6.

Cubes	Flats	Rods	Units
7	2	6	5
− 5	3	9	8

7.

Cubes	Flats	Rods	Units
5	7	0	0
− 4	3	8	2

8.

Cubes	Flats	Rods	Units
8	0	7	6
− 6	2	7	8

9.

Cubes	Flats	Rods	Units
4	0	4	7
− 2	9	3	8

10.

Cubes	Flats	Rods	Units
5	3	0	5
− 3	8	4	5

FIND THE VALUE

Puzzler Pierre came along with his usual puzzlement! He challenged Eager Eddie and Helpful Helen to see if they could find out the value left in these problems. He used the notation (−) to indicate them to "give" the bottom amount.

1.
```
    6  6  7  5
 -  4  5  9  7
```

2.
```
    7  7  5  4
 -  4  8  6  3
```

3.
```
    8  6  8  4
 -  4  7  8  6
```

4.
```
    5  0  6  4
 -  3  7  3  7
```

5.
```
    5  6  0  8
 -  2  7  3  5
```

6.
```
    6  3  7  6
 -  3  4  8  9
```

7.
```
    7  8  0  0
 -  3  4  6  7
```

8.
```
    7  0  6  3
 -  5  3  6  8
```

9.
```
    4  0  5  7
 -  2  3  6  8
```

10.
```
    9  4  0  4
 -  4  8  6  4
```

TAKING ANOTHER LOOK

Puzzler Pierre said to Helpful Helen, "I have a different way of finding out what's left."

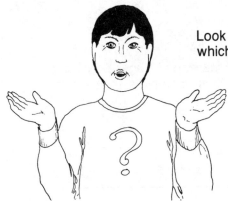

Look at this situation which you write like this:

Cubes	Flats	Rods	Units
4	6	8	5
− 2	5	9	7

"I like to think about combining two things, so I would write it like this:

Cubes	Flats	Rods	Units
4	6	8	5
− 2	5	9	7
		1	1
2	0	8	8

Now to solve it, I would think
What combined with 7, gives me a 5.
⑧ +7=15, so I record a "1" in rods.

Now: 9+1=10, combined with _____ gives me 8. 10+⑧ =18, so I record a "1" in flats.

5+1=6, 6 combined with _____ gives me 6. 6+⓪ =6.

Finally what combined with 2 gives me 4? 2+② =4."

Helpful Helen thought that Puzzler Pierre's method was really "neat," so she decided to try it. Can you help her?

1.

Cubes	Flats	Rods	Units
5	3	7	4
− 2	8	6	9

2.

Cubes	Flats	Rods	Units
6	4	5	3
− 3	7	9	6

3.

Cubes	Flats	Rods	Units
8	6	5	2
− 6	9	8	9

4.

Cubes	Flats	Rods	Units
7	2	0	6
− 5	3	8	8

5.

Cubes	Flats	Rods	Units
5	0	8	7
− 3	2	9	7

6.

Cubes	Flats	Rods	Units
6	9	5	0
− 4	9	6	8

EXCHANGE AND SUBTRACT

Eager Eddie said to Helpful Helen: "Sometimes we have situations where there are none of some pieces. I wonder what it would be like to start with only cubes and then give away some of each type."

"What happens is that you exchange 1 cube for 10 flats, but then exchange 1 flat for 10 rods, and finally you would exchange 1 rod for 10 units.

For example, if you start with 4 cubes, you'd end up with this:

Cubes	Flats	Rods	Units
3	9	9	10

after the exchange.

If you start with 7 cubes; after exchanging you'd have:

Cubes	Flats	Rods	Units

If you start with 8 cubes; after exchanging you'd have:

Cubes	Flats	Rods	Units

With this in mind, let's try these:

1.

Cubes	Flats	Rods	Units
5	0	0	0
− 4	6	8	5

2.

Cubes	Flats	Rods	Units
4	0	0	0
− 2	3	7	4

3.

Cubes	Flats	Rods	Units
6	0	0	0
− 3	4	8	9

4.

Cubes	Flats	Rods	Units
7	0	0	0
− 6	7	2	1

5.

Cubes	Flats	Rods	Units
3	0	0	0
− 1	2	7	4

6.

Cubes	Flats	Rods	Units
4	0	0	0
− 3	8	3	6

7.

Cubes	Flats	Rods	Units
8	0	0	0
− 3	9	0	7

8.

Cubes	Flats	Rods	Units
6	0	0	0
− 5	5	1	4

MORE BORROWING

Suppose we have the following situation:

	Cubes	Flats	Rods	Units
Start	6	7	4	8
Give	3	8	6	9

We can think of this as:

	Cubes	Flats	Rods	Units
Start	6	7 0	4 0	8 0
Give	3	8	6	9

Now, if we started with 6 blocks

	Cubes	Flats	Rods	Units
Start	6	0	0	0
Give	3	8	6	9

We would exchange the 6 cubes

	Cubes	Flats	Rods	Units
Start	5	9	9	10
Give	3	8	6	9
Left	2	1	3	1

But Eager Eddie pointed out that the original value had 6 cubes, 7 flats, 4 rods and 8 units. What we really have left is:

	Cubes	Flats	Rods	Units
	2	1 7	3 4	1 8
	2	8	7	9

SUBTRACT SOME MORE

We can make it easier if we think of how the pattern works when removing numbers from just cubes.

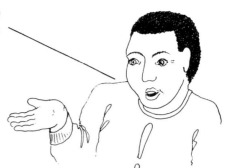

We first remove 5436 from 7 cubes, which we think of as 6 cubes, 9 flats, 9 rods and 10 units

	Cubes	Flats	Rods	Units
Start	6	9	9	10
Give	5	4	3	6
Left	1	5	6	4

Now combine this with the 3 flats, 8 rods, and 2 units we did not use.

Cubes	Flats	Rods	Units
1	5	6	4
	3	8	2
	1		
1	9	4	6

Cubes	Flats	Rods	Units
7	3	8	2
6	9	9	10
5	4	3	6
1	5	6	4
	3	8	2
	1		
1	9	4	6

"Well, let me try:"

1.

Cubes	Flats	Rods	Units
9	7	6	2
5	6	8	4
3	3	1	6
	7	6	2
1			
4	0	7	8

2.

Cubes	Flats	Rods	Units
7	4	6	2
4	3	9	8

3.

Cubes	Flats	Rods	Units
8	6	4	3
5	8	7	4

4.

Cubes	Flats	Rods	Units
9	2	5	4
6	7	9	6

MULTIPLICATION MACHINE

Eager Eddie has a new toy called
a Multiplication Machine.
It looks like this:

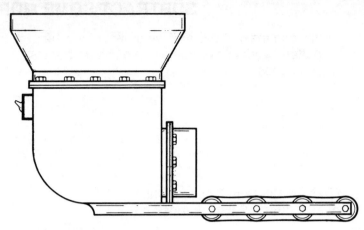

Here's how it works: A number of pieces are recorded in the machine.
Then you feed other pieces into the machine and it gives back pieces.

Watch.

Eddie has recorded a stack of 3 units on the machine.
He feeds it a row of 2 units.

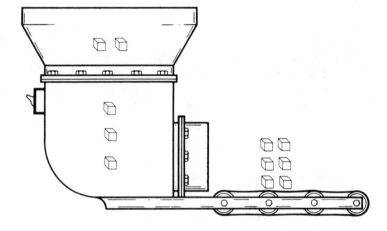

It gave him back _____ rows of _____
units per row, which is a total of _____
units.

Now he has fed the machine a row of 5 units.

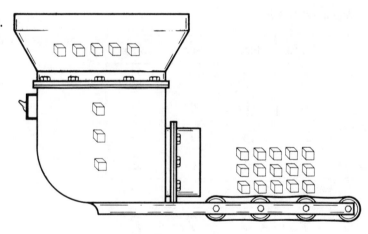

It gives him back _____ rows of _____
units per row, which is a total of _____
units.

Eddie now has recorded a stack of 4 units.
He feeds it a row of 6 units.

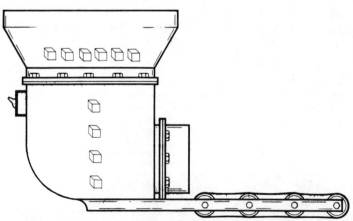

It gives back _____ rows of _____
units per row, which is a total of _____
units.

PRACTICE WITH MULTIPLICATION

1. A stack of 6 units are recorded.
   A row of 5 units are fed in.

   It gives back _____ rows of _____
   units per row, which is a total of _____
   units.

2. A stack of 2 units are recorded.
   A row of 4 rods are fed in.

   It gives back _____ rows of _____
   rods per row. This is a total of _____
   rods.

3. A stack of 3 units are recorded.
   A row of 6 rods are fed in.

   It gives back _____ rows of _____
   rods per row. This is a total of _____
   rods.

4. A stack of 6 units are recorded.
   A row of 3 rods, 2 units are fed in.

   It gives back _____ rows of _____
   units per row, which is a total of _____
   rods, _____ units.

MORE PRACTICE WITH MULTIPLICATION

5. A stack of 4 units are recorded.
   A row of 5 rods, 6 units are fed in.

   It gives back _____ rows of _____
   rods, _____ units per row, which is a total
   of _____ rods, _____ units.

6. A stack of 3 rods are recorded.
   A row of 4 rods are fed in.

   It gives back _____ rows of flats per row,
   which is a total of _____ flats.

7. A stack of 4 rods are recorded.
   A row of 6 rods are fed in.

   It gives back _____ rows of _____
   flats per row, which is a total of _____
   flats.

Try This One
A stack of 4 rods, 2 units are recorded.
A row of 3 rods, 4 units are fed in.

It gives back _____ rows of _____
flats, _____ rods, _____ units per row,
which is a total of _____ flats, _____
rods, _____ units.

62

HELP HELEN

Helpful Helen said to Eager Eddie, "I really like your new toy. I have a group of situations that I'd like to try out."

Can you tell Helpful Helen what the machine would return if the following happened:

1. If I put a row of ▦▦▦ ▢▢ in the machine and there is a stack ▢▢▢ registered,

what would come out? _____

2. If I put a row of ▦▦▦ ▢▢▢▢▢ in the machine and there is a stack ▢▢▢▢ registered,

what would come out? _____

3. If I put a row of ▦▦▦▦▦ ▢▢▢▢▢ in the machine and there is a stack ▢▢▢ registered,

what would come out? _____

4. If I put a row of ▦▦▦▦ ▢▢▢▢ in the machine and there is a stack ▦▦ registered,

what would come out? _____

5. If I put a row of ▦ ▢▢▢▢▢▢▢▢▢▢ in the machine and there is a stack ▦▦▦ registered,

what would come out? _____

6. If I put a row of ▦▦ ▢▢▢▢▢▢▢▢ in the machine and there is a stack ▦▦▦▦ registered,

what would come out? _____

7. If I put a row of ▦▦ ▢▢▢ in the machine and there is a stack ▦▦ ▢▢ registered,

what would come out? _____

MULTIPLYING WITH PIERRE

Puzzler Pierre said to Eager Eddie, "Your toy is O.K., but I have a different way of accomplishing the same thing."

Puzzler Pierre always has to do things differently!

First, I have a code.

• =unit

—— =rod

☐ =flat

=cube

These are used to represent each of the pieces.

Put what you want stacked along the left side and then put the row to be fed along the top like this: Then you can figure out the answer inside.

WATCH!

Now I can count

_____ flats, _____ rods, _____ units

You try it!

_____ flats, _____ rods, _____ units

64

PRACTICE WITH PIERRE

1.

_____ flats, _____ rods, _____ units

2.

_____ flats, _____ rods, _____ units

3.

_____ flats

_____ rods

_____ units

TWO METHODS

Eager Eddie thought Puzzler Pierre's method really worked well, but took up too much space. He suggested that his method could be simplified using a chart.

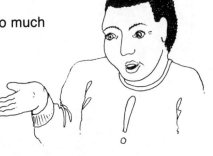

Let's see how these compare:

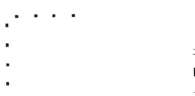

	Rods	Units
		4
Rods		
Units 5		

① 4 units in a row combined with a stack of 5 units, gives me _____ units.

	Rods	Units
	3	
Rods		
Units 5		

② 3 rods in a row combined with a stack of 4 units, gives me _____ rods.

	Rods	Units
		4
Rods 2		
Units		

③ 4 units in a row combined with a stack of 2 rods, gives me _____ rods.

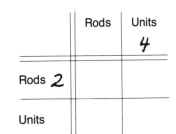

	Flats	Rods	Units
		3	
Rods 2			
Units			

④ 3 rods in a row combined with a stack of 2 rods, gives me _____ rods.

See what happens when you put it together:

	Flats	Rods	Units
		3	4
Rods 2	④	③	
Units 5		②	①
Total			

This would give a total of _____ flats, _____ rods, _____ units.

66

Try solving these problems using Eager Eddie's chart method. If you have problems, use Puzzler Pierre's code and the blocks to help you. The first two problems have some clues to help you!

1.

	Flats	Rods 4	Units 6
Rods 3	④	③	
Units 5		②	①
Total			

① Unit×Unit
② Unit×Rod
③ Rod×Unit
④ Rod×Rod

2.

	Flats	Rods 5	Unit 2
Rods 6	④	③	
Units 3		②	①
Total			

① Unit×Unit
② Unit×Rod
③ Rod×Unit
④ Rod×Rod

3.

	Flats	Rod 4	Units 8
Rod 9			
Units 1			
Total			

4.

	Flats	Rod 4	Units 7
Rod 3			
Units 6			
Total			

5.

	Flat	Rod 7	Unit 2
Rod 6			
Unit 6			
Total			

6.

	Flat	Rod 1	Unit 9
Rod 5			
Unit 7			
Total			

7.

	Flat	Rod 7	Unit 6
Rod 4			
Unit 5			
Total			

8.

	Flat	Rod 8	Unit 3
Rod 7			
Unit 2			
Total			

9.

	Flat	Rod 6	Unit 7
Rod 2			
Unit 8			
Total			

10.

	Flat	Rod 4	Unit 0
Rod 3			
Unit 8			
Total			

Eager Eddie was pleased with the method of using a chart to simplify situations. He decided that one additional step was needed: the Total should be expressed using the fewest number of pieces.

For example, a total of: would be expressed as:

Cubes	Flats	Rods	Units
	15	46	35
1	9	9	5

using the fewest number of pieces.

Your turn:

1.

	Cubes	Flats	Rods	Units
			4	6
Rods 3				
Units 5				
Total				
Exchange				

2.

	Cubes	Flats	Rods	Units
			3	6
Rods 4				
Units 3				
Total				
Exchange				

3.

	Cubes	Flats	Rods	Units
			9	5
Rods 6				
Units 4				
Total				
Exchange				

4.

	Cubes	Flats	Rods	Units
			2	4
Rods 9				
Units 6				
Total				
Exchange				

5.

	Cubes	Flats	Rods	Units
			5	5
Rods 6				
Units 4				
Total				
Exchange				

6.

	Cubes	Flats	Rods	Units
			4	8
Rods 1				
Units 9				
Total				
Exchange				

7.

	Cubes	Flats	Rods	Units
			8	3
Rods 7				
Units 6				
Total				
Exchange				

8.

	Cubes	Flats	Rods	Units
			3	2
Rods 8				
Units 7				
Total				
Exchange				

MISSING PIECES

Helpful Helen told Eager Eddie, "I was playing with your Multiplication Machine and feeding it different rows. It gives me back an amount, but I can't figure out how much is stacked in it. For example, I fed the machine 4 units and it gave me back a total of 12 units. How many are stacked in the machine?"

"Helen, it is easy to figure out. You fed the machine a row of 4 units; it gives you back 12 units arranged in 3 rows with 4 units per row. So, there must be *3 units* stacked in the machine!"

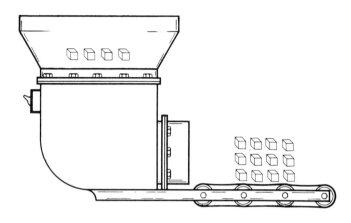

Can you help Helen figure out how many are stacked in the machine in these problems?

_____ units are fed in.
_____ units are given back in
_____ rows of _____ units per
row. So there are _____ units
stacked.

_____ units are fed in.
_____ units are given back in
_____ rows of _____ units per
row. So there are _____ units
stacked.

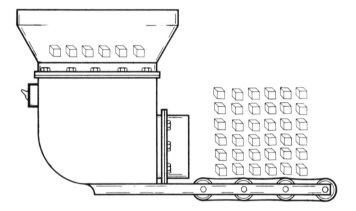

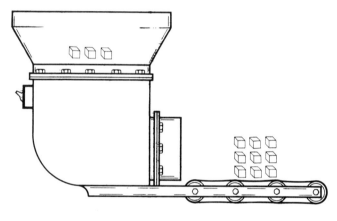

_____ units are fed in.
_____ units are given back in
_____ rows of _____ units per
row. So there are _____ units
stacked.

_____ units are fed in.
_____ units are given back in
_____ rows of _____ units per
row. So there are _____ units
stacked.

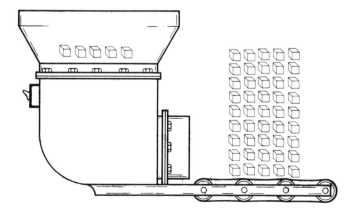

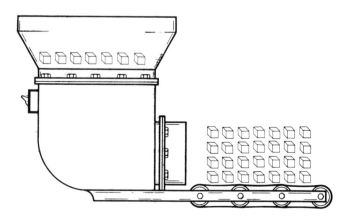

DIVIDING BASE 10 BLOCKS

_____ units are fed in.
_____ units are given back in
_____ rows of _____ units per
row. So there are _____ units
stacked.

_____ units are fed in.
_____ units are given back in
_____ rows of _____ units per
row. So there are _____ units
stacked.

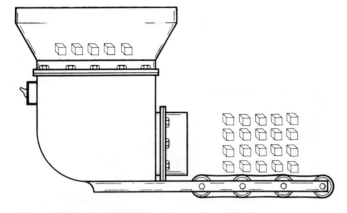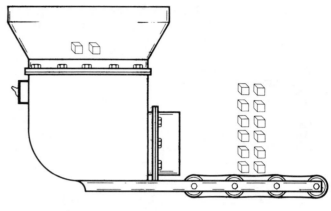

_____ units are fed in.
_____ units are given back in
_____ rows of _____ units per
row. So there are _____ units
stacked.

_____ units are fed in.
_____ units are given back in
_____ rows of _____ units per
row. So there are _____ units
stacked.

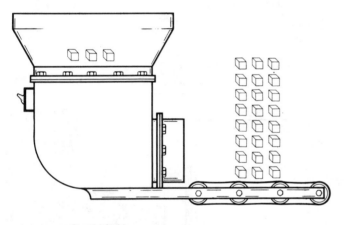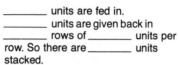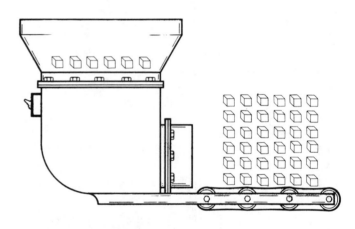

_____ units are fed in.
_____ units are given back in
_____ rows of _____ units per
row. So there are _____ units
stacked.

_____ units are fed in.
_____ units are given back in
_____ rows of _____ units per
row. So there are _____ units
stacked.

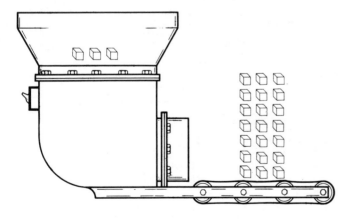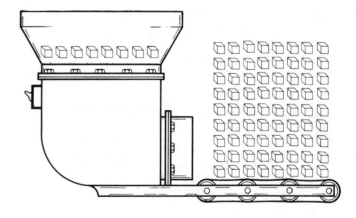

MORE DIVISION

_____ units are fed in.
_____ units are given back in
_____ rows of _____ units per
row. So there are _____ units
stacked.

_____ units are fed in.
_____ units are given back in
_____ rows of _____ units per
row. So there are _____ units
stacked.

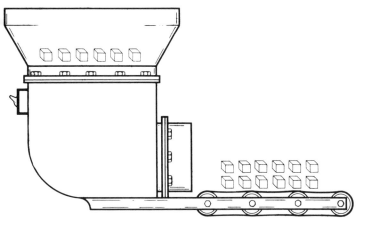

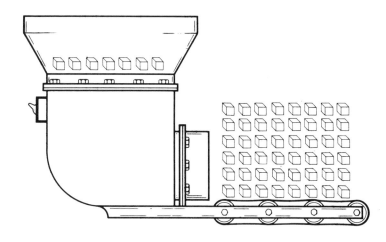

EXTRA FOR EXPERTS

EXTRA FOR EXPERTS

_____ rods are fed in.
_____ rods are given back in
_____ rows of _____ rods per
row. So there are _____ units
stacked.

_____ rods are fed in.
_____ rods are given back in
_____ rows of _____ rods per
row. So there are _____ units
stacked.

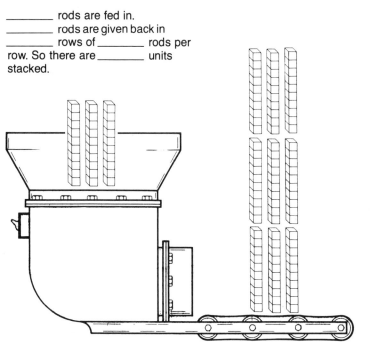

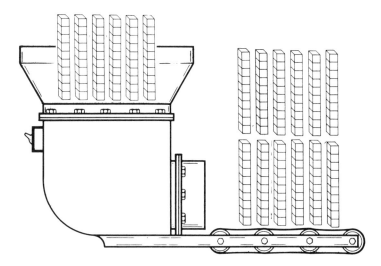

PRACTICE DIVIDING

think

Puzzler Pierre asked Eager Eddie if he could help him out of a jam.

He had

Flats	Rods	Units
4	7	1

that he wanted to share evenly with 3 friends.

The problem was that he couldn't figure out how many each should get.

Eddie said, "Let's look at the situation."

"You have

Flats	Rods	Units
4	7	1

There are 4 flats.

We can give 1 flat to each person...that uses 3 flats
   1 flat per person times 3 people=3 flats

Flats	Rods	Units
4	7	1
3		

It leaves

Flats	Rods	Units
1	7	1

If we exchange the 1 flat for rods, there would be 17 rods.

Flats	Rods	Units
0	17	1

We can give each person 5 rods. 5 rods per person times 3 people uses 15 rods.

Flats	Rods	Units
0	17	1
	15	

It leaves

Flats	Rods	Units
	2	1

If we exchange 2 rods for units, there would be 21 units.

Flats	Rods	Units
0	0	21

We can give each person 7 units. 7 units per person times 3 people uses 21 units.

Flats	Rods	Units
1		

Flats	Rods	Units
1	5	

Flats	Rods	Units
1	5	7

EXCHANGE AND DIVIDE

Pierre said, "Thanks, Eddie. Now I know that each person receives

Flats	Rods	Units
1	5	7

As I was watching you, I realized that we could do this in a single chart—watch:

Share	1	5	7
3	Flats	Rods	Units
	4	7	1
	3		
	1	7	1
		17	1
		15	
		2	1
			21

I start with the fact each person gets 1 flat. I'll record this on top. This uses 3 flats, leaving

Flats	Rods	Units
1	7	1

We'll exchange flats for rods. Each person can receive 5 rods (which we record above). That uses up 15 rods, leaving

Flats	Rods	Units
0	2	1

Exchanging the rods for units, each person can now receive 7 units. That uses up all my pieces. I'll record "7" on top.

We have some more pieces to share. Let's try the above method on them.

TRY TO DIVIDE

Help Puzzler Pierre Decide how many each should get in these situations.

1. Share

4	Flats	Rods	Units
	6	3	2

2. Share

6	Flats	Rods	Units
	7	0	2

3. Share

6	Flats	Rods	Units
	8	2	2

4. Share

5	Flats	Rods	Units
	6	7	5

5. Share

8	Cubes	Flats	Rods	Units
	1	8	8	8

6. Share

3	Cubes	Flats	Rods	Units
	2	3	2	8

74

SHARING BASE 10 BLOCKS

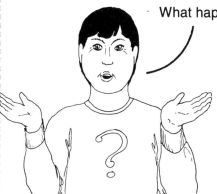

What happens if after I make an exchange, I still don't have enough to share?

Let's look at a problem like that, start with:

Share	0	4	0	6
4	Cubes	Flats	Rods	Units
	1	6	2	4
		16	2	4
		16		
			2	4
				24

One cube cannot be shared among 4 people so exchange for flats show this by placing a zero above.

We now have 16 flats;
each person would receive 4 flats.
4 people times 4 flats per person uses all 16 flats.
Record 4 above.

Now you need to share 2 rods among 4 people, which can't be done. Record a zero above and exchange the 2 rods for units. There are now 24 units. Each person would receive 6 units. 4 people times 6 units per person uses 24 units. Record the 6 above.

MORE PRACTICE DIVIDING

Now I know that if I cannot share after making a trade, I need to record a zero on top.

Try these. Watch for zeroes, sometimes they'll pop up!

1. Share

5	Cubes	Flats	Rods	Units
	1	5	3	5

2. Share

9	Cubes	Flats	Rods	Units
	1	8	5	4

3. Share

8	Cubes	Flats	Rods	Units
	1	5	2	0

4. Share

3	Cubes	Flats	Rods	Units
	4	5	3	3

5. Share

7	Cubes	Flats	Rods	Units
	7	3	5	7

6. Share

6	Cubes	Flats	Rods	Units
	3	6	4	2

HOW MANY?

"Gee Eddie, will your method work if we need to share with more than 10 people?"

"Sure, look at the example I've done for you."

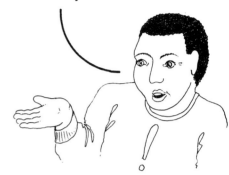

3 cubes cannot be shared evenly among 15 so we need to trade them for flats.

You now have 36 flats. Each person receives 2 flats...record that on top of the chart. 15 people×2 flats per person=30 flats. We are left with 6 flats, 7 rods, 5 units.

Exchange the flats for rods. This gives 67 rods, which allows 4 rods per person when shared. 15 people×4 rods per person=60 rods. Record a "4" on top of the rods column. 7 rods, 5 units are left.

Exchange the rods for units. This gives you 75 units. When 75 units are shared among 15 people, each person receives 5 units. 15 people×5 units per person=75 units. Record the 5 units on top of the chart.

We see that each person gets 2 flats, 4 rods, 5 units.

Share		2	4	5
15	Cubes	Flats	Rods	Units
	3	6	7	5
		36	7	5
		30		
		6	7	5
			67	5
			7	
				75

SOLVE THE PROBLEMS

Don't forget to trade when you have left-overs

1. Share

23	Cubes	Flats	Rods	Units
	8	1	4	2

2. Share

19	Cubes	Flats	Rods	Units
	8	8	7	3

3. Share

36	Cubes	Flats	Rods	Units
	6	0	8	4

4. Share

32	Cubes	Flats	Rods	Units
	6	5	6	0

5. Share

17	Cubes	Flats	Rods	Units
	8	0	4	1

6. Share

36	Cubes	Flats	Rods	Units
	8	2	3	2

INTRODUCING DECIMALS

Let's talk about parts.

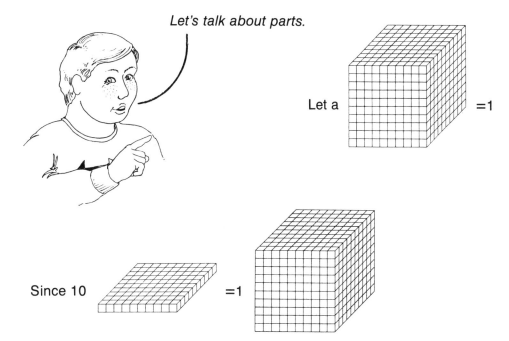

Let a [cube] =1

Since 10 [flat] =1 [cube]

We say each [flat] is one of 10 needed, so each is 1/10 or 0.1 of a cube.

Since 100 [rod] =1 [cube]

We say each [rod] is one of 100 needed, so each is 1/100 or 0.01 of a cube

Since 1000 [unit] =1 [cube]

We say each [unit] is one of 1000 needed, so each is 1/1000 or 0.001 of a cube.

Keep these ideas in mind as you try to answer the questions on the next page...use your blocks to help.

DECIMALS AND FRACTIONS

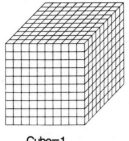

Cube=1
one

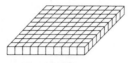

Flat=1/10=0.1
one tenth

Rod=1/100=0.01
one hundredth

Unit=1/1000=0.001
one thousandth

The first few are done for you to give you an idea.

1. 0.3 is the same as _____ hundredths.

2. 0.3 is the same as _____ thousandths.

3. 0.32 is the same as _____ thousandths.

4. 3.2 is the same as _____ tenths.

5. 6.3 is the same as _____ tenths.

6. 6.3 is the same as _____ hundredths.

7. 0.4 is the same as _____ hundredths.

8. 0.4 is the same as _____ thousandths.

9. 5.2 is the same as _____ thousandths.

10. 1.50 is the same as _____ tenths.

11. 0.90 is the same as _____ tenths.

12. 0.230 is the same as _____ hundredths.

13. 0.200 is the same as _____ tenths.

14. 0.123 is the same as 1 tenth+1hundredth+_____ thousandths.

15. 0.34 is the same as 2 tenths+_____ hundredths.

16. 2.5 is the same as 1 ones+_____ hundredths.

17. 3.80 is the same as 3 ones+7 tenths+_____ hundredths.

18. 0.64 is the same as 5 tenths+_____ hundredths.

19. 1.06 is the same as _____ tenths+_____hundredths.

EXPANDING DECIMAL NUMBERS

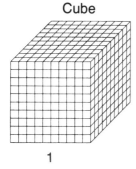

Cube

1

Flat

1/10=0.1

Rod

1/100=0.01

Unit

1/1000=0.001

The number 2.325 is built with:

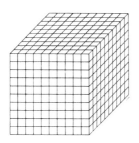 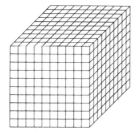 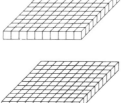 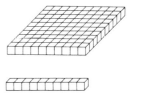

2.325=2 cubes+3 flats+2 rods+5 units
This can also be written as:
2.325=2 ones+3 tenths+2 hundredths+5 thousandths
or   =(2×1)+(3×1/10)+(2×1/100)+(5×1/1000)

The number 1.206 is built with:

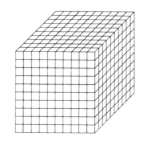 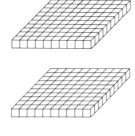

1.206=_____ cubes+_____ flats+_____ rods+_____units

This can also be written as:
1.206=_____ one+_____ tenths+_____ hundredths+_____ thousandths.
     =(____ ×1)+(____ ×1/10)+(____ +1/100)+(____ +1/1000)

Build the following numbers yourself. Record all the different ways of writing the number.

A. 3.4   **C.** 1.235   **E.** 3.069   **G.** 0.234   **I.** 0.307

B. 2.03   **D.** 0.647   **F.** 1.938   **H.** 1.072   **J.** 2.001

BUILDING MORE DECIMAL NUMBERS

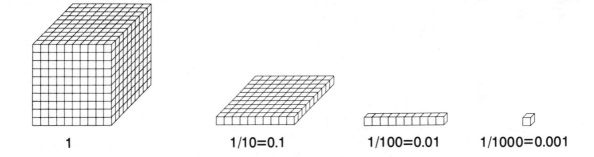

1   1/10=0.1   1/100=0.01   1/1000=0.001

1. Build the following numbers using the fewest blocks.
2. Record the number of cubes, flats, rods and units.
3. List the numbers in order from smallest to largest.

Number	Cubes = 1	Flats = 0.1	Rods = 0.01	Units = 0.001
1.346				
2.42				
1.034				
3.563				
0.004				
0.735				
1.4				
2.035				
0.489				
2.34				
0.07				

MORE PRACTICE WITH NAMING DECIMALS

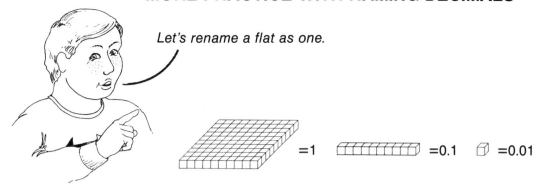

Let's rename a flat as one.

=1   =0.1   =0.01

Since you need 10 rods=1 flat, we say each rod is 1/10 of a flat.

Since you need 100 units=1 flat, we say each unit is 1/100 of a flat.

Determine the number that the picture represents, then write its word name. The first is done for you.

A.

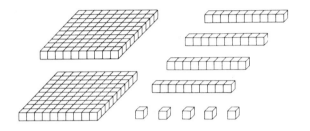

1.45=one and forty-five hundredths

B.

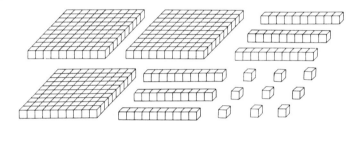

_____

_____

C.

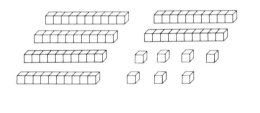

_____

_____

D.

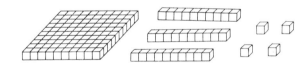

_____

_____

E.

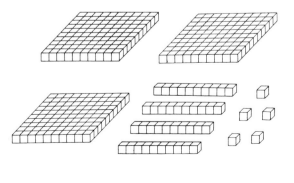

_____

_____

F.

_____

_____

GREATER THAN, LESS THAN, OR EQUAL

Flat

Rod

Unit

1   1/10=0.1   1/100=0.01   1/1000=0.001

Count out the number of blocks in Column I. Make any necessary trades to represent a number using the fewest number of blocks possible. Then compare the number to the number written in Column II. Use the symbols >, <, =.

COLUMN I	SYMBOL >, <, =	COLUMN II
A. 11 rods 16 units number= _____		0.12
B. 17 rods 10 units number= _____		0.18
C. 10 rods 6 units number= _____		0.2
D. 4 flats 14 rods 25 units number= _____		0.0565
E. 7 flats 26 rods 18 units number= _____		0.98
F. 1 cube 8 flats 9 rods 16 units number= _____		1.9
G. 1 cube 8 flats 15 rods 10 units number= _____		1.96

ADDING DECIMALS

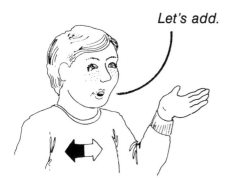

Let's add.

Always Remember that when finding the sum,
the most important thing is to line up your places.

Review thinking steps for addition with Helpful Helen.

We always ask ourselves:
"Are our places lined up?"
"Do we have tenths, with tenths, hundredths with hundredths, thousandths with thousandths?"
"Remember, to start adding the smallest amount first, so you can trade when necessary."

Try these. Build the numbers, then find the sum.

A. 1.35+2.06=

B. 1.3+0.365=

C. 0.47+0.56=

D. 0.704+1.056=

E. 2.36+0.007=

F. 0.963+0.32=

G. 1.481+0.359=

H. 0.58+1.034=

SUBTRACTING DECIMALS

think

Use your blocks to find out how much is left.

Follow Helpful Helen's advice:
1. Line up places
2. Work from smallest to largest place.
3. If necessary, trade and rebuild
4. Fill in zeroes for place holders

The first one is done for you:

Ones	Tenths	Hundredths

2.3
−1.45

Build the top number.

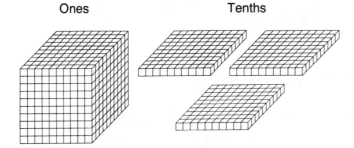

Since there are no hundredths, we trade one tenth for 10 hundredths.

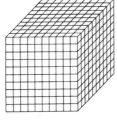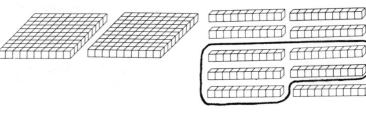

Remove 5 hundredths...
5 hundredths remain.
8 tenths remain.

To remove 4 tenths we need to trade one for 10 tenths...

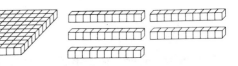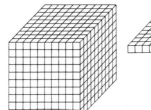

So

  2.3
−1.45
0.85

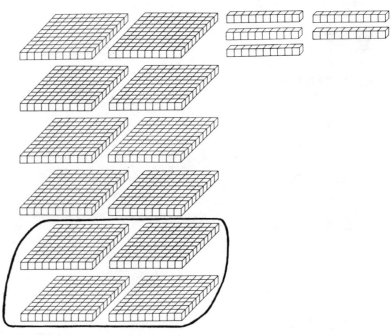

86

SUBTRACTING DECIMALS AGAIN

Study how the problem was completed on the previous page. Then solve these the same way. Rewrite the problem, lining up decimal points.

A. 3.256−1.347=

$$\begin{array}{r} 3.256 \\ -1.347 \\ \hline \end{array}$$

B. 3.23−1.75=

C. 0.563−0.374=

D. 1.45−0.39=

E. 1.673−1.34=

F. 0.278−0.045=

G. 2.346−1.19=

H. 2.32−1.405=

I. 1.2−0.345=

J. 3.0−0.25=

K. 0.563−0.047=

L. 1.96−0.045=

Let a flat=1
Then a rod=0.1
and a unit=0.01

MULTIPLYING DECIMALS

This information will help you solve the following problems.
Build an ARRAY to help.

ARRAY: A rectangular arrangement of a quantity in rows and columns.

Use the pattern of directions in multiplying

3.2

2.1

$$\begin{array}{r} 3.2 \\ \times\ 2.1 \\ \hline .02 \\ .3 \\ .4 \\ 6.0 \\ \hline 6.72 \end{array}$$

.02 ← Multiply 1 tenths by 2 tenths (.1×.2)

.3 ← Multiply 1 tenths by 3 ones (.1×3)

.4 ← Multiply 2 ones by .2 tenths (2×.2)

6.0 ← Multiply 2 ones by 3 ones (2×3)

6.72 ← Total

Let's look at one more

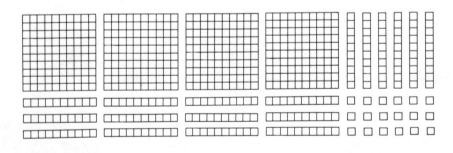

$$\begin{array}{r} 4.6 \\ \times\ 1.3 \\ \hline .18 \\ 1.2 \\ .6 \\ 4.0 \\ \hline 5.98 \end{array}$$

.18 ← Multiply 3 tenths by 6 tenths (.3×.6)

1.2 ← Multiply 3 tenths by 4 ones (.3×4)

.6 ← Multiply 1 one by 6 tenths (1×.6)

4.0 ← Multiply 1 one by 4 ones

Try these

A. 2.3×1.6=

C. 7.3×5.4=

E. 5.6×2.8=

B. 4.6×3.2=

D. 1.4×3.6=

F. 3.9×1.7=

DIVIDING DECIMALS

*A flat is 1
So a rod is 0.1
and a unit=0.01*

In division, we break numbers up into equal groups.

Use your block to help you solve these problems. The first one is done for you.

6.3÷9   Build 6.3 ⟶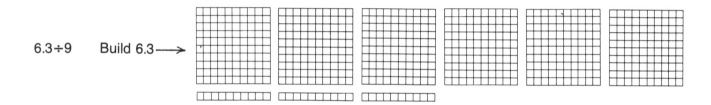

Since there is not enough units to put one in each group, we need to rename 6.3 as 63 tenths. Now we can form 7 tenths in each group.

⟶   6.3÷9=.7

Try these problems; rename when necessary.

A. 2.4÷6=

B. 3.6÷4=

C. 5.6÷8=

D. 6.3÷9=

E. 2.1÷7=

F. 7.2÷8=

G. 1.5÷3=

H. 6.4÷8=

PERIMETER

Perimeter is the distance around a figure.
Help Helen find the perimeter of these shapes by lining up units *around* the outlines of each shape.

Each 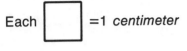 =1 *centimeter*

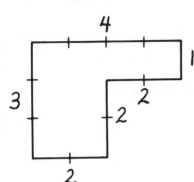

"I need to break the outside up into centimeter units and count the total."

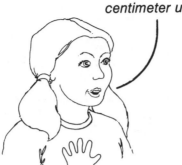

4
3
2
2
2
+ 1
___
Centimeters

A.

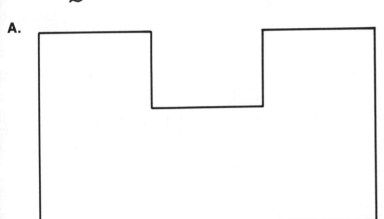

B.

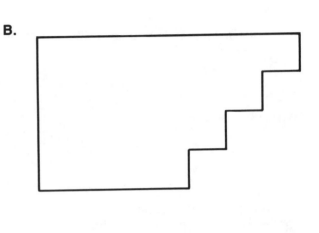

C.

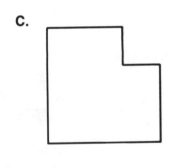

D.

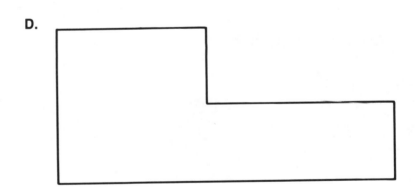

E.

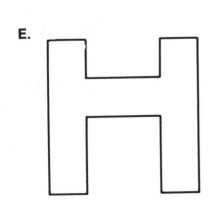

F.

90

AREA

Area is the space a figure covers.

Puzzler Pierre found these tiles and wants to know their area.
Use the units, which are 1 centimeter on each side, to determine the area of each.

Remember, the area of a figure is measured in square units.

The area of this figure is 2 cm²

Tile 1 = _____

Tile 2 = _____

Tile 3 = _____

Tile 4 = _____

AREA

Tile 5 = _____

Tile 6 = _____

Can you find a shortcut for finding area?

Do you need to count by covering with units?

State a formula you can use: _____

EXTRA FOR EXPERTS

A. Eager Eddie wants to buy 6 pieces of Board 2 to build a bookshelf. Puzzler Pierre will sell them for $1.20 per square centimeter. How much will it cost? _____

B. Helpful Helen wants 4 pieces of Board 4 and 3 pieces of Board 6. How much will it cost her at $1.20 a square centimeter? _____

WEIGHT

Let's measure.

1 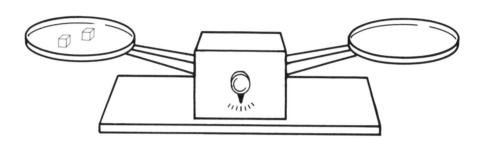 =1 gram

Use your Base 10 Block units to help find
the weight of some familiar objects.

You need to use a balance.

Measure these objects:

OBJECT	WEIGHT
pen	
chalk	
a piece of gum	
your lunch	
a comb	
an eraser	
a pencil	

Find some more objects to weigh.

VOLUME

Volume is the amount of space a figure *occupies*. Volume is measured in cubic units.

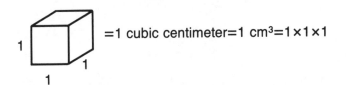 =1 cubic centimeter=1 cm³=1×1×1

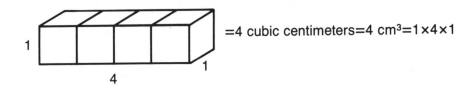 =4 cubic centimeters=4 cm³=1×4×1

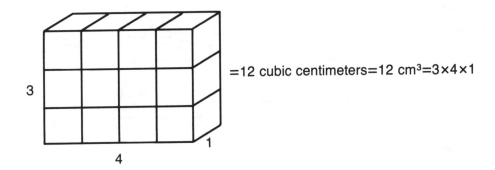 =12 cubic centimeters=12 cm³=3×4×1

Volume is determined by multiplying Length×Width×Height

Build figures having the following measurements; then determine their volume.

A. Length=5; Width=2; Height=3

B. Length=4; Width=8; Height=2

C. Length=6; Width=3; Height=4

D. Length=2; Width=8; Height=3

E. Length=9; Width=8; Height=4

F. Length=10; Width=5; Height=3

G. Length=12; Width=10; Height=4

H. Length=8; Width=10; Height=5

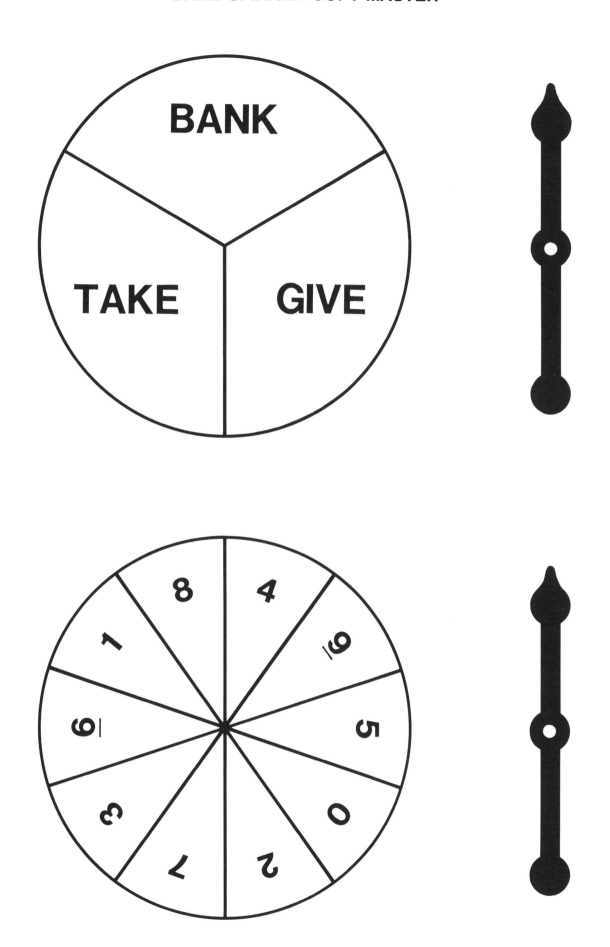